BACKWOODS SURGERY & MEDICINE

BACKWOODS SURGERY & MEDICINE

CHARLES STUART MOODY

ISBN: 978-93-90058-44-0

Published: 1910

LECTOR HOUSE LLP
E-MAIL: lectorpublishing@gmail.com

BACKWOODS SURGERY & MEDICINE

BY

CHARLES STUART MOODY, M. D.

MCMX

CONTENTS

BACKWOODS SURGERY & MEDICINE

CHAPTER I

HOW TO TREAT FRACTURES, SPRAINS AND DIS-LOCATIONS

SEVERAL years ago I stood beside a cot in a hunter's cabin in the heart of the Bitter Root Mountains in Idaho, after a three days' ride, and watched a valuable young life go out as the result of an unattended compound fracture of the thigh. At another time I amputated a leg to prevent the spread of gangrene from a simple cut across the instep while the camper was splitting wood, an accident which, properly treated, would have resulted at most only in a slight inconvenience. Once again, I transformed my boat into a funeral barge and conveyed a young man who had only been in the water three minutes back to his sorrowing parents dead, because his companions were ignorant of how to resuscitate him.

These and many other instances that have come under my observation of the sacrifice of lives from trivial causes, owing to a lack of knowledge, have impressed me with the value of a few suggestions on how to treat the commoner injuries and diseases that may befall those who seek recreation in the remote wilds.

The rules will necessarily be brief and from the nature of things easily followed. The woods loafer should learn them and be prepared whenever the occasion arises. Works on first aid, written ostensibly for the guidance of the laymen, are apt to presuppose a far greater supply of surgical necessities than the hunter cares to burden himself with. It is one thing to apply surgical measures, having at hand a well-filled emergency bag, and quite another to render the same assistance with nothing to depend upon but your native adaptability. My intention is to tell in the plainest and simplest manner possible how to render intelligent assistance to an injured comrade, using only the fewest appliances and those of the most primitive character. These hints are the result of over twenty years of life in the West, in mining camps, cow camps, logging camps, and in the heart of the mountains, where people did not have forethought enough to provide themselves with even a bandage, many times hundreds of miles from where such things could be obtained.

The most appalling accident that can befall a man isolated from skilled surgical aid is the fracture of a limb, especially of the leg, and yet this is one of the commonest of all woods misfortunes.

Before proceeding to the discussion of individual fractures, a brief consideration of the classification and detection of fractures in general is necessary. Surgeons divide fractures into: simple, those where there is a simple separation of the bone without injury to the flesh; compound, where in addition to the separation of the bone there is laceration of the flesh and one or both ends of the bone are driven out through the skin; and comminuted, where the bone is in several fragments. A comminuted fracture may be either simple or compound, according as it does or does not penetrate the flesh.

The symptoms of fracture are pain, loss of motion, change of position, change of contour of the fleshy parts, and most important of all, a light crackling sound when the limb is moved—crepitation the surgeons call it.

Pain following an injury that *might* produce a fracture is not necessarily proof positive of the existence of a fracture. Pain may and often does follow a bruise, sprain, or dislocation, in a greater degree than that following a fracture. Loss of motion, too, is quite as marked in dislocations and severe sprains as in fractures. Change of contour, unless in the locality of prominent joints, is quite a valuable sign. The fractured limb, except in certain rare cases, will show a change in the appearance of its general outline.

By crepitation is meant that characteristic grating sound produced by rubbing the two ends of the fractured bone together. It is the one absolute sign of a fracture, and once heard can never be forgotten. It may be likened to the sound produced by rubbing two or three coarse hairs between the finger and thumb.

If a fracture is suspected let the patient himself, or some one for him, grasp the limb above and below the site of the suspected fracture and turn it in opposite directions. If a fracture is present it will be manifested by a distinct grating sound, also by a jarring sensation as the uneven fragments pass over each other.

A description of all the fractures of the different bones of the body would be manifestly out of place in a book of this character, so I shall confine myself to those most liable to be encountered in the woods—that is, fractures of the leg, thigh, forearm, and arm. Fractures of the leg or thigh will entail an enforced stay of from four to six weeks in the woods, or the devising of some means to transport the patient to a place where he can have proper care, an arduous task in a country where there are no roads and the trails are difficult. If a personal experience may be allowed, I will tell how I once treated a man with fractured thigh and conveyed him with comparatively little discomfort over sixteen miles of rugged mountain trail and some forty miles of equally rugged mountain road.

I found the man in a mining camp in the very heart of the higher mountains, lying in his bunk with a badly fractured thigh. The bone was separated between the upper and middle third—that is, up toward the body. The accident had occurred some twenty hours previous and there was much swelling, which it was necessary to reduce before anything else could be done. This was accomplished by the application of cold water by means of strips of blanket, changing the application as fast as the water became warmed by the body heat.

In the meantime I went out into the timber and felled a small cedar tree some six inches in diameter. From this I cut a section five feet in length and removed the bark. Splitting the bark in half, I rounded up the edges and made a splint for the outside of the limb extending from the armpit to six inches below the foot. The other half was made into a similar splint, only shorter, for the inside of the limb, extending from well up into the groin to a point opposite the outer splint below the foot.

It was necessary to cut holes in the splints where the bony prominences came. When all was in readiness and the limb reduced in size, I wrapped it well in soft cloth, having no absorbent cotton, and applied my splints. I had a man stand at the feet of the injured man, take hold of the injured leg, and pull steadily while I manipulated the fracture.

Right here I want to state that it is unnecessary to try to pull a broken bone out of the socket in order to set a fracture. A persistent pull of some fifty pounds will soon overcome the contraction of the muscles and the bone will be replaced. The acting surgeon must at the same time grasp the limb at the site of the break and knead the two ends into place. You will know when they are in place by the absence of inequality at the point of break.

After the bone had been replaced, I placed my splints in position and bound them on, using strips of sheet torn up for bandages. Any stout cloth will do as well. They may be placed in the ordinary manner, each wrap beside the other, or they may be run on in continuous form, permitting each ascending turn to half overlap the one below it. Care must be taken that the pressure is equal in all parts of the bandage and that it is placed tight enough to prevent any slipping of the splints.

The next problem was to get the man out. Again the cedar forest came to my relief. I felled another and somewhat larger tree, sufficiently large to permit placing the injured man in a boat-shaped section of the bark. This was made longer than his body and a semi-circular board fitted in each end. When the whole was completed it resembled a rude trough.

This trough was lined with blankets until it was quite soft. Two poles twelve feet in length were lashed to either side and the man securely lashed in the contrivance. When we were ready to start two steady pack animals were brought out and the litter with its burden swung in such manner that the animals could wind down the steep rocky trail with the burden between them. In this manner we jogged down the mountainside all day, our patient laughing and enjoying his pipe as though he were the guest of honor in some triumphal procession.

While cedar was mentioned as having been used in the above case, the reader will appreciate that any sort of timber with a tough bark will answer equally well.

There is one important fact that should always be borne in mind in the treatment of all fractures, and that is that at least the two adjoining joints should be fixed. If it is the thigh that is fractured, the hip, knee, and ankle should be included in the splint. If the leg, then the knee and ankle. The same rule holds good with fractures of the forearm or arm.

If timber with tough bark is not available, or in open countries where no timber grows, a broken bone may be nicely splinted by using small round sticks. Never use a clapboard unless it is extremely well padded; even then it is undesirable from the fact that it is liable to press upon some bony point and cause trouble. Also it is very liable to slip and permit your fractured bone to become displaced.

To fix a limb by using round sticks, wrap the limb well in soft cloth; then, having cut your sticks the right length, place them at regular intervals about the limb and bind as before. In the absence of anything better, two leather gun scabbards make quite effective splints.

What has been said with regard to fractures of the lower limb will apply with equal force to breaks of the upper except, of course, that the case is one of far less gravity. In cases of fracture of the arm, either above or below the elbow, the injured person can make himself quite comfortable by pinning the bottom of his coat to his shoulder and placing the injured arm in the V-shaped sling thus formed.

The treatment of compound fractures is one that requires some "nerve" on the part of the acting surgeon and a great deal of fortitude in the injured person. A compound fracture of the leg or thigh is the most terrible accident, short of death, that can befall a man in the woods. Unless great care is exercised the man will die, either shortly from septic poisoning, or almost immediately from shock.

First, get your patient into camp if he is away from it. That may be done in the following manner, which will also illustrate how to carry a person injured in any manner: take a blanket and lay it at full length on the ground; place a pole two feet longer than the blanket directly in the center and fold the blanket over it; lay a similar pole in the center of the folded half and fold the free side back over; place your patient on top, and two men can carry him as comfortably as though he were in a litter. It is, in fact, an emergency litter.

Another emergency litter may be constructed by buttoning an overcoat its full length and running two poles down the sides, laying the patient between them. Failing an overcoat, two short coats or Mackinaw jackets may be made to serve.

Having got your patient with the compound fracture into camp, cut off all clothing from the wounded limb, but no more. It is a bad plan to remove too much clothing from badly injured persons. All the warmth must be conserved, even to the extent of applying artificial heat. Examine the wound for foreign matter and carefully remove it, especially bits of clothing, leaves, small sticks, and bits of earth.

While you have been thus engaged, water should be heated in the cleanest, brightest vessel the camp affords. If there are none bright enough, one may be sterilized by burning it over a hot fire for at least ten minutes. It is absolutely essential that the water used to cleanse a wound of this character should be sterile—that is, without any germ life whatever; hence the directions for boiling it.

In another clean vessel boil all the cloths, towels, and other dressings that you intend using. Any soft cloth will do for dressings, provided it is sterilized and sterilization consists only in thorough boiling.

One of the articles I shall mention in a very limited surgical kit is a bottle of tablets composed of bichloride of mercury known as Bernay's tablets. They are made by all chemical houses and vary in form, but all contain about the same quantity of the antiseptic agent. Some are white and some blue in color, the blue being preferable.

One of these tablets dissolved in a quart of water makes a solution of about the proper strength for dressing wounds. Make your solution and with your sterilized cloths wash out the wound thoroughly, and that does not mean to let a little water flow over the wound; it means to remove every particle of foreign matter in and about the wound.

If the bones have stuck into the earth, as is quite often the case, they must be exposed and the narrow canal cleaned. Then replace the bones in as nearly their proper position as possible. Do not attempt to "set" the bone; just put it back fairly nearly in line. Then cover with several layers of moist cloth that have been previously boiled and dipped in the bichloride solution.

Every day expose the wound, wash it out, and dress it. If the patient is of strong physique and God smiles, he may not have septic fever. If, however, the limb shows signs of inflammation evidenced by swelling and redness, accompanied by fever, chills, and thirst, then must you perform some heroic tasks to save your patient's life.

Remove all dressings and wrap in perfectly clean dressings the entire limb from the hip to the foot, elevate so that it will drain properly, and keep cold water running over it in a small stream constantly. This may be done by making a small hole in the side or the bottom of a bucket and hanging it in such a way that it will permit the stream to fall on the limb. If you follow the foregoing directions implicitly, you have done all that can be done.

It will be understood that what I have said touches upon the subject of fractures in only a very general way. The methods of treatment outlined will apply to practically any fracture, and certainly to those most liable to be encountered in the woods.

The four principal dislocations that are liable to engage your attention are those of the hip, knee, elbow, and shoulder. Of these, that of the hip is the most serious. Without going deeply into the classification of hip-joint dislocation, it will be sufficient to say that fortunately by far the greater number of these is where the head of the bone slips out of its socket upward and backward. Those in which the head of the bone occupies other positions with relation to its socket are much more difficult, in fact, for the layman practically impossible.

The signs of a hip-joint dislocation are shortening of the limb, loss of motion, pain, and the turning of the toes in toward the opposite foot. You will be able to distinguish it from a fracture of the thigh by the absence of crepitation (which I have described as the slight grating sound made by the broken ends of the bone rubbing together), and the fact that in a fracture the toes are generally turned out.

A friend of mine once reduced his own hip-joint dislocation in a manner that may prove instructive. He was coming down the steep side of a mountain in winter on skees. Halfway down the hill, while he was traveling at a great rate of speed, he ran into a depression, breaking his skee and dislocating his hip. It was many miles to the nearest cabin, night was coming on, and it was bitterly cold. Death stared him in the face. It was a time for the exercise of judgment if ever in his life.

He crept down to a grove of small pines, selected two that were just a little farther apart than the length of his body, lashed the foot of the injured limb to one with his pack strap, lay at full length on the snow, and clasped the other with his arms. Pulling with all his might, he had the satisfaction of hearing the bone jolt back into its socket. The idea suggested will enable the reader to modify the method to suit each individual case.

In dislocations of the shoulder the old method still in vogue among some medical men is quite easy of accomplishment. Lay the patient on his back and seat yourself at his side, first having removed the shoe from your foot next to his body. Grasp his injured arm and turn it outward from the body. Place your bare foot well up into his armpit. While an assistant steadies his shoulder, pull downward upon his arm, at the same time moving it toward the patient's body.

Make your pull steady, and when you have begun do not relax until you feel the bone jolt into its position. In the case of muscular persons the pull must be kept up for a longer period, or until the contraction of the muscles has been overcome.

Dislocations of the elbow are usually those in which the two lower bones slip backward and the upper bone forward. They may be reduced by grasping the injured arm just above the elbow with your left hand, the fingers just behind the prominence of the dislocation; with the other hand bend the injured arm well forward, at the same time slipping your left hand downward.

When the injured arm is fully bent, grasp tightly with your left hand at the elbow joint and with your right forcibly straighten it. The fingers of your left hand form a fulcrum for the bone that is out of place to act upon and thus force it back into position. This maneuver is somewhat difficult to describe but quite easy to accomplish. One will be surprised with what ease the bone slips back into position.

Dislocations of the knee are reduced similarly, except that it requires two to do the work. Then, too, the knee often becomes dislocated laterally and the pressure must be made in a lateral direction.

A very distressing little accident is the dislocation of the lower jaw. I once had a patient who rode a long distance with his mouth wide open, suffering a great deal of inconvenience and no little pain, when one of his friends could have relieved him in an instant. Wrap both your thumbs in several layers of cloth, stand behind the patient, who should be seated, and place your thumbs thus protected, on his back teeth, grasp his jaws on either side with your fingers, press down with your thumbs, up with your fingers, at the same time drawing the jaw forward. The bones will go back with a snap and the victim will spasmodically close his mouth hard enough to draw blood unless your thumbs are well shielded.

Dislocations of the joints of the fingers may be reduced by taking a double half-hitch around the finger below the dislocation with a handkerchief, placing your left thumb back of the head of the dislocated bone, and as you pull on the handkerchief with your right hand push forward and downward with your left. The bone will readily slip into place.

Dislocations should be kept at rest for several days and any tendency toward inflammation kept down by the application of water. Severe dislocations, as those of the hip, should be treated similarly to fractures.

Sprains and bruises, while not serious, are often very annoying. When the accident first occurs immerse the limb in cold spring water. This has a tendency to contract the small blood vessels and keep down inflammation. If, however, swelling has already set in, hot water should give place to cold, as hot as can be borne. A consistent application of hot water to a sprain or bruise will ordinarily cure it in a few days.

It may be necessary, under certain conditions, to bandage the limb, especially if one has to make a journey. By applying a roller bandage snugly about a sprained ankle, for instance, one may travel in comparative comfort for several miles. Of course, he will pay the penalty afterwards, but I am speaking now of cases where it is imperative that a man travel.

In applying any bandage be sure that it has no wrinkles in it. It must be laid perfectly smooth and drawn reasonably tight. A loose bandage or one that is placed unevenly is worse than useless.

CHAPTER II

CARING FOR BURNS, CUTS, DROWNING, AND MI-NOR ACCIDENTS

I N speaking of fractures and dislocations I did not dream it necessary to suggest anything in the way of a surgical kit. The element of instruments other than bandages does not enter largely into the treatment of this class of injuries, and the bandages may be improvised from materials at hand.

In the treatment of such wounds as we shall now take up, however, it will be necessary to carry a few things with which to work. This outfit will be limited in its scope, economy of space being imperative. A convenient instrument roll may be made from a strip of canvas, with a pocket at the bottom and loops for holding instruments. This can be rolled into compact shape when filled and tied with tape.

In the pocket place a card of assorted silk ligature, ranging in size from one to six, half a dozen egg-eyed needles ranging from full to half curve, one yard of oiled silk or an equal amount of gutta-percha tissue, one bottle bichloride of mercury tablets mentioned before, half ounce Squibb's surgical powder in shaker-top can, four ounces absorbent cotton in carton, two yards sterilized cotton gauze sealed, a paper of safety pins and another of common pins, one soft rubber catheter, number 9, one roll adhesive tape two inches wide.

In the loops place one needle-holder (Emmet's), one hypodermic syringe (all metal), one pair straight shears about six inches, two hemostatic forceps (Kelly's), one curved bistoury (small), and one splinter forcep. The metal case for the hypodermic has compartments for small tubes containing the hypodermic tablets. Take one tube each of the following: hydrochlorate cocaine gr. 1/4, morphine sulphate gr. 1/4, strychnine sulphate gr. 1/60. With the foregoing rather limited equipment you will be able to render assistance to a person injured in any of the accidents likely to occur in the woods.

There are a few surgical principles that should be impressed upon your mind before the subject of treatment is taken up. The first and most important of these is that it requires a great deal more loss of blood than is popularly supposed to endanger life. There is no danger from hemorrhage from a vein and but little from any of the smaller arteries.

The free flow of blood from a wound instead of being alarming is the most beneficial thing that can happen. The cleansing power of flowing blood cannot be overestimated and it is cleansing that all wounds require. That brings up a second thought. All serious consequences arising from incised or punctured wounds come from the invasion of bacteria, and all your efforts should be directed against these energetic little gentlemen, either those that have already entered the wound or those that are striving to gain ingress.

A simple cut will, if permitted to seal itself up in its own blood, generally heal without any further interference. The man who puts tobacco, flour, soap, or any other of the popular monstrosities on a wound is little short of a criminal.

While, theoretically, many people know that blood flowing in a steady stream is coming from a vein and that flowing in jets or spurts is coming from an artery, few know how to take advantage of that knowledge. The general rule to make pressure between the heart and the wound in case of a jet and between the wound and the extremity in case of a stream is only good as a general rule; there are exceptions and it is exceptions that make the rule dangerous. There are times when it becomes necessary to reverse the process.

The proper way is to make compression with your fingers until you have located the region the blood comes from; then apply your steady compression in that locality. There are a few great arterial trunks that lie near the surface and may become injured, the injury causing death from hemorrhage. The manner of locating the compression point for these arteries will be given.

The first of these is the great artery that runs down the inside of the leg, called the femoral. Bleeding from this vessel will result in death in a very few minutes, and it has been known to be severed by a man falling on his sheath knife. The bleeding may be controlled by grasping the leg with the fingers near the body. About half way down the inner surface of the leg the fingers will fall into a slight depression, at the bottom of which lies the femoral artery.

Any of the vessels of the lower limb may be controlled by compressing just behind the knee between the two prominent tendons that will be found there when the leg is doubled up. Arteries of the forearm and hand can be stopped by pressing with the thumb at the elbow joint just to the inner side of the tendon of the biceps which you may feel like a cord when the arm is extended. If the bleeding is from the upper arm stretch the whole arm by raising it above the head. Feel in the armpit and you will locate a prominent ridge on the inner side; press with your fingers just behind that ridge and you will shut off the blood supply from the whole arm. These are the more prominent vessels that lie near the skin.

Certain of these larger arteries require ligation. The ligation of an artery calls for a certain amount of surgical skill, but if it is necessary to save life you can do it. Surgeons now use sterilized catgut for the purpose, but silk can be used as well, taking care to leave sufficient end hanging out of the wound to remove it by.

After having made compression and controlled the hemorrhage, clean out the wound and loosen your tourniquet until the blood spurts. Locating the artery, grasp it in the bite of the hemostatic forceps. Cut off a short piece of silk and tie it loosely around the forceps. Have some one pull up on the forceps and at the same time with your forefingers slip the knot down over the end of the cut vessel. Tie tight and remove your forceps.

This procedure will be necessary only in case of injury to large vessels. Smaller arteries can be controlled by the means hereafter described, or by placing a heavy pad of gauze over them and making compression with a tight bandage. The blood will become entangled in the meshes of the cloth and form a clot.

Incised wounds inflicted with sharp instruments will be found to comprise practically all the injuries occurring in the woods. The method of treating one will illustrate that of dealing with all. Let us suppose that in cutting firewood the camper has had the misfortune to drive a sharp ax into his instep (a quite common accident). The blood spouts at once in a very alarming manner. He hobbles to the camp and removes his shoes. An ugly gaping wound appears, from the bottom of which blood is jetting, indicating that an artery has been severed.

The first thing necessary is to stop the blood. Take a handkerchief or other cloth and tie it about the ankle rather loosely, place a small stick or a table fork beneath it and twist. In a few turns you will note that the blood is flowing with less force and shortly will cease altogether.

When the bleeding has been entirely controlled get out your surgical kit and throw a pair of the hemostatic forceps into the boiling water. After they are sterilized wash the wound free from blood with pure water. I will add in this connection that spring water in the mountains is practically sterile and can be used for washing wounds without any danger of infection.

After the wound is clean have some one slightly loosen the tourniquet. As he does this watch sharply for the jet of blood that will locate the cut artery. As soon as you see it grasp it with the forceps, lock them, and leave them in place. The compression of the forceps while you are getting ready your other instruments will seal up the vessel so that when you remove them it will not bleed any more.

Take two of your full curved needles, at least two inches long, and thread them with quite coarse silk, cut off a piece of your gauze and run the needles through it. Place the needles thus prepared, the needle holder, shears, and the other pair of hemostats in a vessel and boil. In the meantime make up a solution of the bichloride, using the antiseptic tablets for that purpose.

Wash your hands well and rinse them in the bichloride solution. Clean out the wound, taking great care to remove all clots. With one of the threaded needles in the grasp of the needle holder begin at the upper angle of the wound, about half an inch from the end. Pass the needle down through the flesh one-fourth of an inch from the edge, carrying it well toward the bottom and making it enter the wound near the bottom and re-enter the flesh on the opposite side, pass up through and out an equal distance from the edge. Cut the thread off and lay the two ends out of your way, leaving, of course, sufficient to tie with when the time comes.

Place your row of stitches half an inch apart all down the wound. When all the stitches are in place you may begin to tie. Take the two ends of the first stitch in your hands and lift up on them; this will bring the edges of the wound together. Tie the thread, turning the first knot under twice to prevent its slipping. After all the stitches have been tied take the handle of your scalpel or the forceps and raise the edges of the skin, which will have rolled in, until they meet each other. This is necessary, as where the skin is rolled in it will not heal readily and leaves an opening for the entrance of bacteria.

Sponge off all the free blood and dust well with surgical powder. Place a pad of gauze that has been soaked in the bichloride solution over the wound, cover that with a wad of cotton and the cotton with a piece of oiled silk, bandage over all, and do not molest for at least three days.

After five days you may remove your stitches in this manner: Cut the stitch near the skin on one side, grasp the knot in the bite of the forceps and pull it out. Be careful not to try to pull the knot through the flesh, and do not leave any end on the part you do pull through the flesh, as it may carry infection down into the wound.

It is a fact not generally known to the laity that a solution of common salt and water will take the place of blood when introduced into the system. Surgeons resort to this practice in performing all very bloody operations. Their method of hypodermoclysis could not be carried out in the camp, of course, but a very good substitute for it can be used. The lower bowel is very receptive of this solution, which by the way, is made by dissolving a teaspoonful of clean common salt in a pint of water. The solution, maintained at blood heat, is introduced into the lower bowel with a fountain syringe. Persons who have lost a great deal of blood, so much in fact that their pulse can hardly be felt at the wrist, will receive great benefit from this procedure. Use at least a gallon of the solution and do not permit it to flow too rapidly into the bowel.

Certain cuts may be dressed without stitches. Proceed as before up to the point of putting in the stitches, then roll up two pieces of gauze as long as the cut and about the size of a lead pencil. Lay these on either side of the wound quite close to it. With adhesive tape half an inch wide and four inches long begin two inches on either side of the wound and carry across, bringing the edges of the wound together. Place these strips half an inch apart until the wound is brought into line. Dress as before, except that you will have to omit the moist gauze, dressing with the powder entirely.

I want to add here that should you run out of sterilized gauze at any time you can make it from any soft cloth by boiling it for ten minutes in the bichloride solution and hanging in the air to dry.

The pain attendant upon any surgical manipulation can be prevented by the hypodermic injection of a solution of cocaine. When you get your hypodermic have the instrument man show you how it works. He can show you much better than I can tell it. Insert the needle half an inch from the wound and inject a few drops of the solution into the skin. Proceed thus entirely around the wound and by the time you are through the wound will be perfectly painless. Before replacing the instrument in its case always dry it out and replace the small brass wire that you will find in the needle.

It is somewhat difficult to approach the subject of punctured wounds, which also include those resulting from gun shots and powder explosions. The rule among surgeons is to meddle with these injuries as little as possible, provided they do not penetrate the abdomen. In the case of penetrating wounds caused by falling on a sharp stick or other sharp pointed instrument, it is well to clean out the wound, removing all foreign substance that may be present, searching diligently for pieces of cloth, rust, charcoal, bark, or other foreign matter. These things in certain localities contain the germ of lock-jaw, and many contain it anywhere.

This is particularly true of felt wads from shotgun shells. All diligence should be exercised to clean out a wound resulting from such a cause. Shotgun wads are manufactured from the most filthy kinds of old hair, often reeking with the bacillus of tetanus.

If the wound was caused by a sliver of wood and the sliver still remains in the wound remove it by making an incision with your bistoury. Do not be afraid to cut. A little cut is worse than none; go deep enough to liberate the sliver so that it may be removed with the splinter forceps. Then wash the wound from the bottom with hot water and dress as before, using the bichloride.

Experience has proved that the less one attempts to do with gunshot wounds the better. Nature has a tendency to wall off foreign bodies that are in the main sterile and will ordinarily do so with a bullet if given a chance. Keep the patient quiet, prevent infection from entering the wound, and trust to Nature to do the rest.

An incident will illustrate what takes place when Nature is given an opportunity to throw out her plastic wall material around a foreign body. Some years ago a party of Eastern people were camping in the heart of the Bitter Roots. Among the party were two boys of the age when boys are prone to try experiments. They bored a small hole in a spruce tree and drove into it a high power 30–30 cartridge. Then they stood off some fifteen feet and fired at the cartridge with a small rifle. One of them hit it.

The 30–30 shell came back and penetrated the abdomen of the juvenile marksman, burying itself and driving pieces of clothing into the abdominal cavity. The messenger who came for me was thirty-six hours on the trail and I was an equal length of time reaching the camp. The people had had sense enough to keep the patient quiet and I found him resting fairly easy. So deeply had the missile penetrated that it required a considerable incision to remove it.

When I reached the bottom of the wound I found that Nature had thrown about the wounded area a wall of protective lymph and all the pus that had accumulated was in a pocket. I laid the pocket well open, evacuated its contents, and removed the bits of cloth that I found, dressed the wound, and had the satisfaction of seeing the youngster recover.

Burns are classified according to degree of injury. Those of the first degree are where the skin is reddened, but no blister formed. The second degree includes those where there has been decided blistering, and the third, where the flesh has been charred. Those of the first and second degrees are the most common in about the proportion of 99 to 1.

A burn of the first degree can be best relieved by the application of cold water.

This is contrary to the teachings of a few years ago, but is in full accord with that of to-day. The water should be changed as fast as it becomes warm.

Burns of the second degree require more care. In the first place, do not interfere with the blister. The primary object in treating burns is to exclude air and the skin remaining intact will do this much better than any artificial means.

The Indians of the Northwest prepare a dressing for burns by cooking deer suet with balm of gilead buds. This is the most effective application for severe burns I have ever seen. If deer suet is not available, any fresh tallow that has been cooked will serve as well. Throw a handful of the buds into a vessel and cover them with the suet, boil for thirty minutes, and strain. When nearly cold apply to the burn and cover with a soft cloth. The pain ceases almost immediately.

It seems singular after all that has been written on the subject, but few people know how to restore a drowned person. The matter is really quite simple, yet it requires great attention to detail. Spasmodic efforts are useless. The thing has to be gone about methodically and the method persisted in for a long time, often in the face of seeming certain defeat.

In the first place, statistics show that no person who has been submerged in the water for a period of seven minutes was ever resuscitated. It is extremely doubtful if after five minutes' immersion anything can be accomplished, still it is worth the effort.

The first thing to do when a person is rescued from the water is to remove all clothing from about the chest and neck. Do not take the time to draw the garments off, but rip them off with a knife. Turn the body over and stand astride it. Grasp it about the middle and lift up so that only the head and feet are touching the ground. This is done in order to free the lungs and air passages from water and mucus. Do this several times.

With a handkerchief wipe out the mouth and as far down the throat as you can reach. Lay the patient on his back with a folded coat under his shoulders. Kneel at his head and grasp both arms at the wrists and pull them well up over his head, hold for an instant, return to the sides and press them against the ribs, hold for an instant and repeat. Do this about twenty times each minute.

The tendency is to work too fast. The movement should be about as fast as a man breathes, the object being to simulate the ordinary respiratory movements as nearly as may be. While this is being done another person may grasp the tongue and pull it up and out of the mouth, keeping time with the movements of the arms. When the patient begins to show signs of life wrap him well in hot blankets, place hot stones at his feet, and administer hot water, brandy, or strong hot coffee.

As before suggested, the efforts at restoration should be persisted in for a long time, until either success rewards your efforts or the body becomes quite cold and rigid. It may be that there is a little spark of life left and you may fan it into flame after hours of effort.

There are many minor accidents for which it is well to be prepared. For example, to remove a fish hook. Do not try to pull it back; push it on through, file or break off the barb and it can be removed readily.

To remove foreign bodies from the eye: First cocainize the eye by dropping a few drops of a solution made by dissolving one of the cocaine tablets in a half teaspoonful of water, then turn the lid back over a match telling the person to look down at the same time, and brush the substance off with a soft cloth. If it is under the lower lid place your forefinger on his cheek just beneath the eye, pull down, and tell him to look up. If it adheres to the eyeball, as in the case of a cinder or a small piece of steel, after cocainizing the eye remove with a sharp knife by brushing.

Insects sometimes crawl into the ear and make a lot of commotion. Place the patient on his side with that ear uppermost and pour plenty of warm water into the ear. By plenty I mean several quarts. The bug will crawl out or be washed out by the returning stream of water.

Burns well characterized toothache as "Thou hell of a' diseases." If the tooth has a cavity (as it probably has), a small crystal of cocaine dropped dry into the cavity and covered with a little pledget of cotton will give immediate relief.

For bleeding from the nose, place a pledget of cotton in each nostril, lay the patient on his face, and pour cold water over the back of the neck. Leave the cotton there for several hours. The idea is that the fibrin in the blood becomes entangled in the fiber of the cotton and sets up a clot that seals the bleeding surface, while the cold water closes the blood supply by its action on the artery supplying the parts.

Hiccough is a distressing and sometimes a dangerous complaint. Many times a swallow of water will stop it. If simple measures fail, the following has been found very efficacious. The nerves that produce hiccough are near the surface in the neck. They may be reached and compressed by placing two fingers right in the center of the top of the breastbone between the two cords that run up either side of the neck and pressing inward, downward, and outward. A few minutes' pressure of this kind will stop the most obstinate hiccough.

Certain injuries are attended with what is known as shock. Usually the degree of shock is proportionate to the extent of the injury, though not always so. Often seemingly trivial injuries produce a fatal shock. The symptoms are cold, clammy skin, face very pale and pinched, eyes widely dilated and staring, pulse rapid and irregular, little or no pain, even from severe injuries. The patient retains his mental faculties but loses the power to originate, answering when spoken to but usually volunteering no statements of his own.

The treatment consists in lowering the head and elevating the extremities. Wrap the patient in hot blankets and place hot water bottles about him, give brandy, or what is as good, hot water; inject 1/30 gr. strychnia every fifteen minutes for three doses.

The symptoms from loss of blood are very much the same as from shock and luckily respond to the same treatment. In addition, if there chances to be a fountain syringe in the camp, give rectal enemas of hot normal salt solution, which can be made by dissolving a teaspoonful of common salt in a quart of sterile water. In some way this solution seems to take the place of the blood lost. A hot application over the heart is also valuable, as are mustard drafts to the spine.

CHAPTER III

MEDICAL TREATMENT OF CAMP DISEASES

I N this day of compact pharmaceuticals one can carry a complete equipment of medicines in a vest pocket almost. The old day of ponderous powders and nauseating liquids has passed. The physician now who prescribes for his patients immense bottles of "shotgun" mixtures writes himself down a back number. This manner of administering drugs can be taken advantage of by the man who wishes to carry with him upon his outing a supply of remedies for the relief of such ailments as may befall him.

Oliver Wendell Holmes once said in delivering an address to the graduating medical class of Harvard, "Young men, you have been taught here at least twenty remedies for every disease; after you have practiced medicine twenty years you will have one remedy for twenty diseases."

The genial autocrat was nearly right. The longer one continues in the practice of medicine, the fewer remedies he learns to depend upon. An Irish medical friend of mine once put the thing in very apt form when he said, "If I had to practice medicine on an island where I could have only three remedies, I should choose castor oil, opium, and strychnia. I'd physic them with the castor oil, constipate them with the opium, and stimulate them with the strychnia."

These remarks are a little beside the subject, but I am constrained to quote them to illustrate that but few medicines are needed, if these be well understood, and the indications for their use can be mastered by anyone in a short time.

For the past several years my emergency medical case has contained only ten remedies, and with these I have not hesitated to make professional trips of many miles. The case should be made of sole leather with a pocket for a small note book and loops for a clinical thermometer. The bottles should hold half an ounce and have screw caps. Have the glazier etch with his diamond the numbers from 1 to 10 on the sides of the bottles. The reason for this is that numbers pasted on are liable to rub off, and as many tablets look much alike confusion may occur. Then fill them in this manner:

No. 1: Calomel, gr. 1/4. Make this entry in the little note book that is contained in the pocket. "No. 1, calomel gr. 1/4. Dose, one tablet every thirty minutes for four hours. Indications, biliousness, headache from disordered stomach, diarrhea, colds, and the beginning of all fevers."

No. 2: Dosimetric trinity (Full strength). Dose, one granule every half hour until skin becomes moist. Indications, all fevers, colds, threatened pneumonia, and threatened typhoid.

No. 3: Chlorodyne. Dose, one tablet every hour to relief. Indications, any gastric pain, cramps, diarrhea (after cleaning out the bowels), colic, acute indigestion.

No. 4: Intestinal antiseptic. Dose, one tablet every hour for four hours; then one every three hours. Indications, after bowels have been cleaned out to correct any disorder of the tract, as a routine treatment of typhoid; always valuable in diarrhea and other inflammatory conditions of the bowels.

No. 5: Quinine sulphate, gr. 5. Dose, one tablet every four hours. Indications, colds and catarrh, bilious fevers, specific in malaria.

No. 6: Elaterin, gr. 1/16. Dose, one tablet. Indications, to remove all fermenting food matters in the stomach and bowels, produces excessive watery evacuations. Valuable in dropsy; especially applicable where you want to get rid of the entire contents of the bowels.

No. 7: Phenacetine, gr. 5. Dose, one tablet every three hours to profuse perspiration. Indications, reduce fever where pulse is full and bounding. Relieves headache; taken early cures severe cold.

No. 8: Sun Cholera. Dose, one every three hours. Indications, similar to No. 3, only more powerful, valuable in severe summer complaint due to eating fresh fruit, meat, drinking too much water. Relieves gastric pain.

No. 9: Apomorphia hydrochlorate, gr. 1/10. Dose, two tablets followed by swallow of hot water. Indications, as an emetic in poisoning. Use cautiously.

No. 10: Digitalin, gr. 1/100. Dose, one tablet every hour to effect. Indications, the most powerful heart tonic and reconstructive. Must be used cautiously. Valuable in loss of blood, excessive heart action from altitude, and all conditions where heart is not performing properly.

It will be noted that I did not mention morphine, strychnia, or cocaine, as they were spoken of in connection with the hypodermic. In the case I also place a one-minute clinical thermometer. All of these instruments are now made self-registering and must be shaken down after each using. This should be done, not by a jar, but with a long sweep of the arm. Too sudden a jar will snap the instrument in two. Shake until the mercury column stands below the △ mark. This △ mark indicates the body heat at normal condition, that is, 98.4° F.

Every man should familiarize himself with certain physiological facts, and with these as guideposts he ought to be able to follow a train of indications to a reasonably fair diagnosis. The pulse rate, taken at the wrist, is generally a fair index of the condition of the body. The normal man has a pulse rate of about seventy-two beats per minute, women somewhat more rapid; high elevations also produce a more rapid pulse.

If there is an increase of heart beat above eighty per minute, accompanied by other subjective symptoms, it is an indication that something is wrong. In the absence of a clinical thermometer, one can arrive at a pretty fair knowledge of the body heat by counting the pulse. It is estimated that there will be an elevation of one degree F. for every ten beats above the normal. This rule varies, but is a fair average.

The appearance of the tongue is a valuable signpost, but one that is difficult of mastery. A few prominent indications will be noted. A thin, white, even furring of the tongue is indicative of gastric disturbances and mild fever states. A flabby, swollen, indented tongue covered with a uniform yellow, pasty fur is indicative of profound gastric states and gastro-duodenitis; it may also be produced by a continued moderate fever.

A narrow tongue, with deep median fissure on each side of which is a thick rough fur, the tip and edges being red and denuded, is characteristic of typhoid states whether arising from typhoid or not. The same condition will be found in profound intoxication from septic poisons. If the tongue becomes dry and brown, tremulous when protruded, and the patient returns it slowly when requested to do so, he has typhoid beyond question. A brown fur on the root of the tongue, especially in the morning, indicates a sluggish condition of the liver. In jaundice the tongue is yellow.

It is estimated that the normal man in a state of rest will breathe sixteen times per minute. Any radical departure from the rate will indicate disease. An increase of two respirations per minute is supposed to indicate a rise of one degree F. in the body temperature, though this rule is subject to variations. Inspection of the bare chest tells the trained physician much regarding the condition of his patient and even the layman can glean much knowledge from that source.

If the patient is breathing from twenty-five to thirty-five times per minute, the respiration being confined to one lung as indicated by the lack of expansion in the other, and if he lies so as to take the strain off the lung that does not expand, it is almost sure that the patient has pneumonia. In case the lung is fixed rigidly by the muscles and the opposite lung forced to do all the work, then the patient has pleurisy.

In profound typhoid states the breathing is very much slowed and irregular, at last presenting what is known as the Cheyne-Stokes respiration, in which the patient will breathe several short shallow respirations, pause for a time, heave a deep sigh and then repeat the rapid breathing. This type of breathing is looked upon as a very grave symptom in all conditions characterized by lack of physical strength.

It will be readily appreciated that only enough discussion of symptoms has been given above to aid somewhat in arriving at a diagnosis. To go deeply into physical indications of diseases would be manifestly out of place in an article of this character. We will now proceed to the consideration of the diseases that will be most frequently encountered in the camp. Of these the intestinal troubles stand pre-eminent. Change of water, food, methods of life, and personal habits account for the fact that nearly every person who seeks the outdoors at some time during his stay is afflicted with some one of the diarrheas. Without attempting to go deeply into the various classifications of the enteric complaints, a brief résumé of the guiding symptoms common to all will be given.

It matters very little so far as the treatment is concerned whether it be an ileo-colitis, an ileitis, or simply colitis. The same treatment would obtain in each case, and the same general trend of symptoms would be present. The patient feels a general indisposition, loss of appetite, headache, and sleeplessness, which is followed by pain and griping in the bowels; then comes the diarrhea, which may be profuse and watery or scanty and accompanied by much pain. The evacuations become exceedingly frequent, sometimes as many as fifty or sixty per day.

The patient vomits frequently and is quite ill, his face becomes pinched and dusky, with an anxious look in the eyes. There is some fever and thirst, though the water drunk is generally vomited. In the above has been pictured an extreme case of summer diarrhea. There will be all gradations below this, from a mere soreness of the abdomen and looseness of the bowels up to profound prostration from constant drain on the system induced by the evacuations.

By a sort of strange medical paradox, in order to stop the evacuations it becomes necessary to increase them. We must sweep out the nest of troublesome bacteria that are causing the disturbance. An ordinary cathartic will not accomplish this. It is necessary to administer something that will produce a profuse watery discharge from the bowels. Nothing accomplishes this better than a heaping tablespoonful of Epsom salts in hot water, but as we have not provided for such bulky medicines in our case we will give our patient one tablet of elaterin which will accomplish the same purpose.

Then, too, the patient is not nearly so liable to vomit the elaterin. If he does, however, the vomiting can be controlled by the administration of cocaine by the mouth, though this latter drug must be used very cautiously. A tablet of 1/4 gr. cocaine hydrochlorate given in a swallow of hot water will stop vomiting until the other remedies can produce their effect. Before giving any other medicines await the free action of the cathartic.

The patient should have at least three very copious discharges; then begin to combat the inflammatory condition that exists in the bowels. The chlorodyne tablet will in all ordinary cases, do this best of all your remedies. There will be some few instances where it will be necessary to resort to more powerful remedies; in that case the Sun Cholera tablet given according to directions is the best. As an after treatment in these cases the intestinal antiseptic gives the best results. A tablet every four hours for two days will annihilate every vestige of bacterial invasion that may remain.

Bronchial and pulmonary diseases supply a large percentage of the camp ailments in the fall and early winter during the deer hunting season. An attack of pneumonia following a severe drenching from being out all day in a rain, or accidentally tumbling into the creek, is not a pleasant thing to contemplate. It usually comes in the night. The patient wakes out of a sound sleep with a chill. There is a sharp sticking pain as though a knife were being thrust between the ribs, at some point on the chest wall. The breath comes in short gasps and the patient instinctively turns toward the affected side in order to ease the pain.

The chill may or may not be followed by vomiting, and the fever lights up immediately, rising to 102–4° F. A distressing short cough comes along to add to the discomfort as each act of coughing increases the pain in the chest. In less than twenty-four hours the patient begins to expectorate what we call "prune-juice" mucus, that is, mucus streaked with blood until it resembles the juice of cooked prunes. When you see this "prune-juice" you need have no doubt as to the diagnosis. You should, however, have been busy long before this.

There is no doubt now among educated physicians that pneumonia, taken in time, can be aborted. When the pain first manifests itself set somebody to baking hot cakes made from flour stirred with water. While these are still as hot as can be borne lay them over the painful spot on the lung, renewing as fast as they become cool. To accomplish much good this treatment must be kept up until the period of expectoration and even after, at least twenty-four hours. At the same time begin by administering calomel in 1/4 gr. doses every thirty minutes until at least three grains have been given.

Two hours after the last tablet of calomel has been given, give a tablet of elaterin. When the latter has "worked," start in with the dosimetric trinity tablets and push them until the skin becomes moist and the fever falls below 100° F. Do not give any of the coal tar products in pneumonia, that is, do not give phenacetine or acetanilide. When the patient is recovering it is well to keep up the heart by strychnia or digitalin.

There is such a thing as giving too much of these heart stimulants though, and you should watch the pulse closely. Stimulating the heart too greatly is liable to cause congestion of the small blood vessels in the lungs and defeat the very purpose you set out to accomplish.

Taking "cold" is a very popular camp method of feeling bad. The man who does not at least once, while in camp, stuff himself full of a good old-fashioned "cold" feels that he has been cheated out of a part of the enjoyment of his outing. For the benefit of those of his companions who do not appreciate his "barking" in season and out, the following rules are suggested: First, take a bath; it may be painful but necessary. Second, assist overworked eliminants to remove the debris that has accumulated by reason of the failure of the ordinary processes of waste removal.

This can be done very nicely with a heroic dose of calomel; by heroic about three grains is meant. Follow up the calomel with several five-grain doses of phenacetine, or until the patient is in a profuse perspiration, roll him in warm blankets, and await developments. A careful observance of the foregoing will annihilate any able-bodied "cold" on earth.

The man who contracts rheumatism in camp has my sincere sympathy. It requires no special skill to tell when one has it, but it does require special powers of divination to tell when he will get rid of it. Medical science has discovered only one drug that will affect the progress of the disease in the least, and that only after an extended course. Salicylic acid in one or another of its various combinations furnishes the sheet anchor in the treatment of rheumatism. I purposely omitted it from our pocket case of drugs because of the fact that the combination that would suit one man's stomach would not another.

In practice we have to take many things into consideration in the administration of the salicylates. The man with rheumatism in camp can seek only to relieve the pain and assist Nature to eliminate the waste. A thorough flushing of the bowels should be the first thing, followed by aconitine, gr. 1/134, one tablet every hour for four hours; then one every three hours. At the same time keep dry. If it be a limb that is affected wrap it in blankets and "cook" it in front of the fire.

Cases of poisoning arising in camp will usually be confined to two causes— the eating of poisoned foods and eating poisonous mushrooms. In these days of tinned meats and vegetables it is not unusual to hear of persons becoming seriously and even fatally poisoned by eating certain canned goods. Canned fish and beef are the worst offenders in this regard.

The symptoms of ptomaine poisoning are characteristic and generally easily traced to the material producing them. There is a dryness and metallic taste in the mouth shortly after eating suspected food. This is followed by severe cramps, vomiting, violent purging, rapid loss of strength, great depression and coldness of the surface of the body. The hands and face break out in clammy sweat and the temperature falls below normal. The picture is very characteristic and when once seen is readily recognized.

The treatment consists in getting rid of the offending substance as quickly as possible. Nothing accomplishes this more readily than a quick emetic. Apomorphia hydrochlorate furnishes us with the most convenient emetic, though mustard water or hot salt water will do. Take a tablet of 1/10 gr. apomorphia hypodermically, or two tablets of the same size by the mouth, followed by a swallow of hot water. Hypodermically the emetic acts in a very short time; by the mouth it requires somewhat longer, say ten minutes. Purge the bowels with elaterin, one tablet, then keep up the vital forces by administering strychnia, 1/60 gr. every hour or two, watching the circulation meanwhile.

In severe cases, in addition to the strychnia, it may become necessary to resort to external heat, hot water bottles, hot stones, etc. The patient is much debilitated for several days and requires careful diet.

Mushrooms should never be eaten unless the person gathering them is known to be thoroughly conversant with the different varieties. Certain poisonous varieties resemble the edible so closely that only an expert can tell the difference. The knowledge, however, is one that every hunter and camper should familiarize himself with as mushrooms are usually plenty in the hills and furnish an agreeable addition to the menu.

Phalline, the toxic principle of the *phalloidæ* group of mushrooms, is a toxalbumin of extreme violence and resembles very much the toxic albuminose of rattlesnake virus; in fact, it seems to act upon the digestion very much as crotalin does upon the circulation. There is another toxic principle present in certain other varieties of fungi called muscarine; both these poisons act very similarly.

The symptoms are a feeling of giddiness coming on from one hour to fifteen hours after eating the fungus. This is followed by profuse salivation, the water running out of the patient's mouth in a stream. Blindness ensues, and vomiting and diarrhea come in their train. The heart is weakened and the patient breathes with difficulty. At the last he lies in a stupor.

The treatment is similar to that of ptomaine poisoning. Remove the offending material at once by the same process. For a purgative oleaginous agents are the best if available, castor oil being preferable; failing in that any active cathartic will do. The heart then must be stimulated by the digitalin; strychnia also plays a prominent role here.

It had not been my intention to mention typhoid, but upon reflection I have decided to include it. Typhoid fever is little liable to attack people living under such conditions as exist in the mountains where the air is pure, the water comes from eternal springs, and flies are few. Summer camps along lake shores and the larger, slow-moving streams are liable to it, and it is just as well to recognize it when it arrives.

The person about to come down with typhoid generally feels extremely tired for several days, the head and back ache, the nose frequently bleeds slightly, a rumbling is present in the right side just below the ribs, and the ears rings as though one had taken an overdose of quinine. The tongue is characteristic of the disease, so much so, in fact, that we speak of a particular condition as the "typhoid tongue."

After a few days the patient begins to feel feverish. All the symptoms increase until he is quite ill and takes to his bed. About this time tiny red spots called "rose spots" appear on the abdomen, perhaps only a few, again they are quite frequent. The mind becomes dull and the hearing imperfect.

Typhoid is said to be a self-limiting disease, that is, it cannot be cut short or aborted in any way. That, however, is hardly the case. By vigorous treatment, at the outset, it is now thought by a great many that the disease can be limited to a few days. If the treatment is not begun early and carried out, the disease will run a course of some twenty-one days.

The treatment consists in eradicating the nest of typhoid bacillus that is setting up the disturbance. Here, again, we resort to calomel. Four grains given in quarter-grain doses every half hour will usually produce sufficiently free passages. After this administer the intestinal antiseptic religiously, with aconitine for the fever. Give plenty of water to drink and restrict the diet. If the disease gets beyond control, the routine treatment is the intestinal antiseptic.

Cold packs for the fever, in the later stages of the disease, will be found preferable to any medicines. All the time the diet should be watched. No solid foods should be allowed. Milk, light broths, fruit juices, and rice water supply sufficient nourishment and do not irritate the tender glands of Peyer and Brunner that are the seat of the disease. These glands become very friable in typhoid, and any violent action of the walls of the intestines, as in digesting food, will cause them to break through and permit the bowel contents to enter the general peritoneal cavity, when the patient will die from inflammation of the bowels.

CHAPTER IV

SERPENT WOUNDS AND THEIR TREATMENT

EVERY summer outdoor America leaves the heat and dust and turmoil of the city for the peace and quiet of the wild. Doubtless many persons penetrate, in their outing, regions where venomous serpents abound. These will carry as a part of their equipment remedies intended for the relief of wounds inflicted by these. Many of these remedies will be absolutely valueless for the purpose intended, and many more will fail from lack of intelligent application. A brief discussion of serpents and the approved methods of treating their wounds may prove of interest at this time.

Permit me to state at the outset that such information as may be contained in this chapter is not the result of conjecture and guesswork, but is derived from over twenty-five years study of reptilian zoölogy, many years investigation in the laboratory, during which time an extended series of experiments were carried out, and twelve years' actual practice, in which all of the methods that have suggested from time to time have been thoroughly tested.

There are, roughly speaking, something like twenty-eight varieties of venomous reptiles in the United States. These figures include the one lizard that is known to be poisonous and the several scorpions. Of this number the rattlesnakes comprise at least eighteen. In fact, so important are they that all others may be included in a discussion of the crotalidæ; more particularly so as all serpent venoms act chemically in the same manner.

Man is unreasoningly afraid of snakes. It is rare, indeed, that a person concerns himself with the classification of the serpent that chances to cross his path. He immediately possesses himself of a stout club and proceeds to maul the unoffending reptile into the earth without troubling his mind to find out if the snake is harmless or otherwise. This is wrong, for when one comes to know them serpents are quite interesting. It is wrong, too, for with a little study the ordinary man can familiarize himself with the characteristic markings of the venomous serpents and differentiate them from those that are non-venomous.

All the deadly snakes, with the exception of the little harlequin snake of the extreme South, are similarly marked and all belong to the class of "pit" vipers, characterized by a depression or "pit" back of the nostril. The head is triangular, with massive muscular development of the jaw; the neck slender in proportion to the size of the head and body. The body itself is quite thick, the skin rough. The pupil of the eye is elliptical instead of being round as in the non-venomous snakes.

The harmless varieties, on the other hand, are long and slender, the skin smooth and shining, the head oval or round. If in doubt after the above, the investigator can pin his subject to the ground with a forked stick placed just back of the head and examine the teeth. If he finds, hanging from the upper jaw, or inclined forward from it, two fangs, long and sharp as needles, he can be pretty safe in assuming that his subject is poisonous. The non-venomous snakes have a dentition very much the same as some of the smaller rodents, the mice for instance.

The habitat frequently furnishes a key to the character of the snake. The venomous varieties choose by preference the rocky uplands, either open or sparsely wooded. The harmless snakes live almost exclusively in low swampy lands or along water courses. Venomous snakes are purely terrestrial. One was never known to ascend a tree. In fact it is impossible for one to do so.

While rattlesnakes are dangerous, their bite is not nearly so fatal as is popularly supposed. This fact has at least two important reasons, viz., season and the habits of life of the snake. In the extreme South and in midsummer the venom attains its highest state of virulence. Then the person fairly struck by a large rattler is in extreme danger, provided the second factor in the equation does not intrude, that is, the habits of life.

All venomous snakes, and more especially rattlesnakes, are sluggish. They do not move rapidly or over great distances. Their lethal power is given them as a means of procuring food and when once the snake strikes he expends practically all the ammunition in his arsenal. It requires hours and perhaps days to renew the supply, during which time the serpent is defenseless. Should the human victim happen along at such time and be bitten it is quite probable that he would not receive a fatal dose of the poison.

The manner in which the rattlesnake inflicts his wound is worthy of some study. In the first place, it may be assumed as axiomatic that the snake cannot strike farther than his own length and seldom even that. Stories of rattlesnakes lifting themselves from the ground bodily and hurling themselves through the air are purely imaginative. Nor can the snake strike unless coiled. It does not follow that he must be in complete coil, but he must have at least a few kinks in his spine before he can deliver a blow; then he can only strike the length of the kinks.

If permitted he will assume full coil before striking and when undisturbed he lies in that position. The maneuver of assuming full coil takes longer than is generally thought. Writers who assert that the snake can throw himself into full coil instantly are far from the truth. In fact it takes, on an average, something like five seconds for him to get his length in position to deliver his most powerful blow. My experiments have developed another interesting fact, that the snake cannot strike an object held directly over his head. It must be held at an angle.

How deep will the needle-sharp fangs penetrate. That depends, too, upon conditions. A large snake, striking from full coil, will naturally drive his fangs much deeper than another smaller, striking from a less advantageous position. Upon the bare flesh the snake will sink his fangs to their full extent. His blow, however, is often delivered with a raking motion and the wound inflicted resembles the scratch of a briar.

Certain articles of dress are less permeable than others. Rubber, even thin rubber, is wellnigh impenetrable. Soft, closely woven cloth is also resistent. In experiments I have placed blotting paper behind two thicknesses of heavy flannel and only in rare instances have I found the virus staining the paper. This fact will serve to inform the reader that the ordinary protection of the lower limbs will be adequate to shield the wearer in a rattlesnake country.

The chances of being bitten, even in a country abounding in snakes, are really quite insignificant. The rattler is the most inoffensive gentleman of my serpentine acquaintance. He is perfectly willing, if you will permit him, to lie all day basking in the sun upon some convenient rock and never molest the passer in the least. If he has sufficient warning he will slip quietly out of your path and give you the right of way. He only strikes when in his reptilian mind he deems himself insulted or in danger.

An extended discussion of the chemistry of serpent venoms would be manifestly out of place at this time. We owe practically all our knowledge upon the subject to the painstaking efforts of two men, S. Weir Mitchell and Prof. Reichert. These gentlemen gave to the world almost simultaneously the result of their labors. The lethal principle of all serpent venoms consists of two elements, a venom peptone and a venom globulin.

These elements are albuminoid in character, and it is interesting to note that they act no differently from the pure albuminoses of digestion. One element has the power to destroy the fibrin ferment in the blood, the other acts as a paralyzant upon motor and sensory nerve trunks.

Time has no effect apparently upon the poisonous quality of these venoms. After twenty years' preservation in glycerine Dr. Mitchell found the virus as active as ever, and it is known that arrows steeped in rattlesnake venom retain their power for many years. Heat in varying degrees, or a sudden violent application of it, will destroy the poisonous property, as will also absolute alcohol.

The action of the virus on the animal economy is interesting and worthy of study. When taken into the circulation the symptoms are quite characteristic and not easily mistaken, even by the man of no scientific training. This is well, as the wound itself is insignificant and might be overlooked. In fact, I have known many persons to be bitten and not know it until the symptoms apprised them of the fact.

A stinging, burning pain radiates from the wound and the wound itself becomes inflamed and angry. Swelling comes on, the heart action is immediately accelerated, and the respiration hurried. In a short time, as the virus penetrates deeper into the systemic circulation, the heat and respiratory symptoms change, the heart slows down, the respiration decreases, the face becomes dusky and anxious, covered with profuse perspiration, and the mind grows dull. Blindness, due to the effect upon the optic nerve, takes place.

The patient staggers as he walks, and soon, unless relief comes, he will become totally paralyzed. Spots of blood appear just beneath the skin and especially upon the limb bitten. If the amount of the virus is sufficient to produce death, all the above symptoms are soon followed by tetanic convulsions and lockjaw. If, however, the dose is not sufficient to produce death, they gradually subside, leaving the patient much debilitated and subject to poisoned blood states that manifest themselves in the form of skin eruptions and ulcers.

The reader will appreciate that in the above has been pictured an extreme case. Nothing like nearly all cases bitten present even half the symptoms described. Statistics reveal that only something like 12 per cent. of all persons bitten by the New World venomous serpents die from their wounds.

Before passing to a consideration of the means for combating a poison let us pause for a time and glance at the probabilities of being struck even in a country where venomous serpents abound. The "rim rock" of the Columbia River in Washington and Oregon is an ideal place for rattlesnakes and they abound there in profusion.

Children run barefoot all summer among the basaltic rocks, and but few of them are bitten. Haymakers fork them up with the haycocks, harvesters find them beneath the bundles of bound grain, still it is rare to hear of an accident. Among the "brakes" of the Clearwater in Idaho the great "timber" rattler dwells. The Indians never molest him, yet during my nine years' sojourn among them only seven cases appeared, and two of these were very young children.

Still, people are bitten, and the location of the wound has much to do with the chances of recovery. About 60 per cent. of all persons wounded are struck on the lower limbs, thirty-five on the hand or arm, and five on the trunk and face. Of these, wounds on the lower limbs are the least dangerous and those on the trunk or face, being near large nerve and arterial vessels, most so. The more remote from the general circulation, the less danger from the wound.

The treatment of a rattlesnake wound resolves itself into the application of a few very simple rules. In the first place a person wounded by a snake usually does the very thing he should not do—that is, goes tearing off at top speed for the nearest human habitation, thereby increasing the circulation and disseminating the virus through the system more rapidly. The man should sit calmly down and bind his handkerchief around the limb (if it is a limb), break off a stout twig and insert beneath the handkerchief, producing a rude tourniquet, and twist until the circulation is effectually shut off.

With a sharp knife make an X incision over the wound, taking care to penetrate deeper than the fangs have done. If he has good teeth and no canker in his mouth, he may now suck vigorously upon the wound. It does no good to suck the original wound. It is quite difficult to get any virus back through an opening not greater in caliber than a fine needle.

If all this is done without delay, the chances are that the patient will suffer no great inconvenience from his experience. If he chances to have handy a stick of silver nitrate he can cauterize the wound thoroughly. Failing that, a brand from the fire will serve. After a time he may release his tourniquet somewhat and permit a portion of the retained blood to enter the circulation; the system is capable of tak ing care of a great deal of poison if it is allowed to flow into the blood gradually.

If, however, the virus has been permitted to enter the circulation at once the case is one calling for radical measures. In this connection it is well to state that alcoholics defeat the end required. The time-honored belief in the efficacy of whiskey in the treatment of rattlesnake bites is pernicious in the extreme. Alcohol, like serpent venom, has two effects, the later or depressant effect being exactly the same as the depressant effect of the venom itself. Therefore the man who recovers from a rattlesnake wound after drinking a large quantity of whiskey does so in spite of his remedy, not with its aid.

The one sovereign remedy in these cases is strychnia, and no man should penetrate a snake country without having this valuable adjunct with him. The administration of strychnia is not so difficult but that any man of ordinary intelligence can inform himself about it in a short time. It is a powerful alkaloid, of course, and must be applied with intelligence to accomplish the end desired. How much to administer will depend upon the person and the character of the wound.

It must be taken into consideration that the system already poisoned by the venom will tolerate a larger quantity than one in a normal condition. The average dose of strychnia hypodermically applied is 1/30 of a grain. This may be increased to say 1/15 grain without any serious danger. A person suffering from rattlesnake venom will bear without danger perhaps 1/2 grain or even more.

It will be understood that this amount is not to be thrown into the blood all at one dose, but spread out over an interval of thirty minutes. Strychnia has its most important field in the treatment of these cases after the depressant effect of the venom has taken place. The rule then should be to administer until the heart approximates the normal. The patient can take too much, then again he can take too little.

Chemical antidotes directed against the venom of serpents are extremely problematical. It is questionable if there is at present any chemical that will exert more than an antiseptic effect upon the virus. Permanganate of potassium may possess the property of setting up a chemical reaction, but if so it is so prone to deteriorate when in solution and requires so much time to place in solution that it is nearly valueless.

Ammonia applied to certain of the less dangerous venoms is efficacious. Applied to crotalus poison it is of no use. In fact, when the matter is reduced to its lowest terms, the whole process of combating the effect of serpent venoms is comprised in what has been stated above. Restrict the circulation, destroy the virus by heat either chemically or by fire, and keep up the vital forces. Very few Indian tribes have any suggestion of a remedy for rattlesnake poison. The Moquis probably have, though if so no white man has ever been able to extract the secret from them. It is known that during the Moqui Snake Dance many Indians are bitten and none of them die. It might be inferred then that they do possess an effective antidote.

In conclusion permit me to suggest an equipment for the treatment of rattlesnake wounds and briefly outline its uses. Procure a rubber ribbon about four feet long, technically known as an Esmarch tourniquet—this ribbon can be rolled into a compact form and is very elastic—; a sharp surgeon's knife known as a bistoury which should be securely wrapped in absorbent cotton; a blue bottle, or one about which several thicknesses of blue paper have been wrapped, containing a stick of silver nitrate; another bottle containing one hundred tablets of strychnia sulphate gr. 1/30; an all-metal hypodermic syringe for administering the same.

All these should be placed in an oiled silk bag and kept in a convenient pocket. The bag should be changed when the clothing is changed just the same as the watch or compass.

Now for their use: Let us suppose that you have encountered a rattler and are not too scared to know what you are doing. You quietly sit down, expose the limb, locate the wound, get out your Esmarch and beginning at one end wrap it securely about the limb *above* the wound, gradually increasing the tension until the rubber sinks into the skin.

This done, take your knife and make a deep X over the wound, using the cotton in which the knife was wrapped to sponge away the blood. Encourage free bleeding. If you are near a stream bathe the wound freely, either squeezing or sucking it. You need not fear to swallow the poison. It will do no harm in the stomach. After the wound has bled freely, take the stick of silver nitrate and burn it out quite to the bottom. All of this will hurt, of course, but it is necessary.

The administration of the strychnia will follow next in order only if the depressant symptoms of the venom indicate its need. Should the patient feel the approach of the dizziness that is the beginning of the stage of paralysis, he should then think about his strychnia. Dissolve one of the tablets in warm water and fill the barrel of the syringe; screw on the needle, first removing the fine wire that runs through it. Plunge the needle into the fleshy part of the arm at an angle of about ten degrees from the horizontal and push home the plunger. Repeat this every fifteen minutes until the heart Has returned to the normal.

These directions closely followed will save every case of rattlesnake bite, and in many instances the patient will not require the strychnia at all. The wound made by the knife will require the same general treatment as any other simple wound.

THE CAMPER'S MEDICINE CHEST

Surgical Supplies

One instrument roll, 80 cents.

One paper medium size safety pins, 10 cents.

One paper medium size common pins, 5 cents.

One-half dozen assorted gauze bandage, size one-to three-inch; 10 cents each.

Two yards sterilized plain gauze in carton, 20 cents yard.

Four ounces sterilized absorbent cotton in carton, 20 cents.

One roll three-inch adhesive plaster, $1.

One-fourth dozen silk ligature braided, in glass tube fitted with half curved needles, 30 cents a tube.

One card braided silk ligature, assorted on one card (white), about 30 cents.

One-half dozen assorted egg-eyed surgeon's needles, half to full curve, 50 cents.

One ounce Squibb's surgical powder, 50 cents oz.; or a like amount of camphophenique powder, $1.

One hundred Bernay's antiseptic tablets (blue), 25 cents.

Two five-inch hemostatic forceps (Kelly's), about $1 each.

One pair straight, sharp-pointed surgeon's shears, about $1.25.

One needle holder (Emmet's), $2.50.

One splinter forcep, may be used also for dressing forcep. This forcep should neither have mouse tooth jaws nor serrated jaws, and should run to a fine point; 50 cents.

One hypodermic syringe, all metal, in metal case, $1.50.

One one-minute clinical thermometer in metal case; will cost about $1.25, according to reliability. The best registered instrument is cheapest.

One number 9 soft rubber catheter, 25 cents.

One cake surgical soap, in metal box, 75 cents.

The above will comprise practically everything that may be found absolutely necessary. With them the ingenious man can perform practically every minor surgical operation that he would care to undertake. If he cares for a more elaborate outfit he may add the following:

One yard oiled silk, in tube, 75 cents.

One pure rubber fountain syringe, $1.75.

Four ounces creolin, in metal screw-cap bottle, 25 cents oz.

One or more first aid packages at 50 cents per package.

One emergency tourniquet, $1.25.

Eight ounces carron oil for burns, 25 cents oz.

The size of the surgical outfit will depend, of course, upon the size of the party. The dressings and things that will be destroyed will necessarily have to be increased in proportion to the number of the party.

Medical Stores

The suggestions here will be based upon a party of four staying one month.

In the case with the hypodermic place one tube strychnia sulphate, gr. 1/30, price 20 cents. Use as a powerful stimulant hypodermically one tablet every four hours, if needed, watching the action of the heart carefully. One tube cocaine muriate, gr. 1/4, price 50 cents. Use as a local anesthetic as suggested in chapter on surgery and for toothache. Can be used to control vomiting—one tablet followed by swallow of hot water every four hours, if needed. Solution of one tablet in spoonful of hot water dropped in eye to deaden so as to remove foreign bodies. One tube morphine sulphate, gr. 1/4, and atropine sulphate, gr. 1/100, combined, price 25 cents. Use as a sedative for pain, one tablet hypodermically repeated every two hours to effect; digitalin, gr. 1/100, price 25 cents. Use as heart stimulant where action of heart is deranged, one tablet not oftener than thrice daily. One tube apomorphia hydrochlorate, gr. 1/10, price 50 cents. Use to induce vomiting in cases of poisoning, one tablet hypodermically only. One tube glonoin, gr. 1/100, price 15 cents. Use as heart stimulant in shock and great depression due to cerebral anemia; not in loss of blood, however.

One sole leather medicine case with screw-cap glass bottles, numbers etched on bottles, price from $1 to $3, according to style and finish.

Book to slip in pocket for keeping list of remedies and their therapeutic application, cost 25 cents.

The bottles filled as follows: The numbering need not adhere strictly to that here given:

No. 1. Aconitine gr. 1/134. 200 at 25 cents per C. Use in cases of high fever where heart is full and bounding and there is great congestion as shown by headache, backache, etc. Use in beginning of all colds. Take in all cases one tablet every fifteen minutes for an hour then one tablet every two hours, or better still take every half hour until pulse becomes soft and surface of skin is moist.

No. 2. Dosimetric Trinity No. 1. 200 at 50 cents per C. One tablet every half hour to effect. The effect will be to reduce all fevers much the same as above except that it may be continued over a longer time and becomes a routine treatment in typhoid, pneumonia, grippe, bronchitis, rheumatic fever, and in all cases of fever where the heart seems to need a slight stimulation.

No. 3. Intestinal antiseptic. 500 at 50 cents per C. One tablet every three hours as routine treatment in typhoid, diarrhea, colic, dysentery, and all disordered fermentative conditions of the intestinal tract.

No. 4. Quinine sulphate, gr. 5, either in tablet or capsule form, cost about 10 cents a dozen; take 100. Use in malaria, one tablet every four hours during attack and not less than fifteen grains daily as a preventative. In decidedly malarial countries this amount will have to be taken daily, consequently the amount carried should be materially increased. Is somewhat valuable in colds, bronchitis, etc.

No. 5. Sun Cholera. 100 at 50 cents per C. One tablet every four hours in cases of watery diarrhea, after bowels have been cleaned out by purgative. Of use also in colic, flatulence, intestinal pain.

No. 6. Chlorodyne. 100 at $1.00 per C. Take one tablet every two or three hours in extreme pain, vomiting from fermentative processes, summer diarrhea, etc.

No. 7. Calomel, gr. 1/4. 200 at 10 cents per C. Use one tablet every thirty minutes or every hour for eight doses, in all cases where bowels need thorough cleaning out. As beginning treatment in all cases of fever, vomiting, diarrhea, in fact about everything that happens.

No. 8. Phenacetine, gr. 5. 100 at 50 cents per C. One tablet every four hours to reduce fever as in colds, some forms of dysentery, and in severe headache. To be discarded when case bids fair to become prolonged.

No. 9. Elaterin, gr. 1/16. 25 at one cent each. Use one tablet only where it is necessary to secure an immediate watery passage from the bowels in order to sweep out offending masses.

No. 10. Dover's powder, gr. 5. 100 at 50 cents per C. Use one tablet every four hours in sudden acute colds. Its most valuable field is in the colds and bronchitis of children. Continue until perspiration ensues.

In case the medicine case holds more than ten bottles the additional bottles may be filled with brown mixture, 100 at 25 cents per C. One tablet every four hours to one three times a day in cases of indigestion, flatulence, "sour stomach," etc.

Headache tablet consisting of acetanilid, sodium salicylate, ammonium bromide. A choice tablet to be given every four hours where persons are subject to congestive headaches. The least objectionable of all the "coal tar" tablets. These may be had at about 25 cents per dozen, and the case should contain at least 100 of them.

Tonsilitis tablet consisting of menthol, thymol, phenol, potash, chlorate, and sodium chloride. Take 200 at about 25 cents per 100. Use as a gargle in tonsilitis, sore throat, and pharyngitis. Dissolve tablet in half pint hot water and gargle several times a day.

It will be noted that in the above unnumbered list aconitine and Dover's powder have been substituted for apomorphia hydrochlorate and digitalin recommended in Chapter III. Either list is good, and will be found comprehensive for all ordinary emergencies.

THE END.

Lector House believes that a society develops through a two-fold approach of continuous learning and adaptation, which is derived from the study of classic literary works spread across the historic timeline of literature records. Therefore, we aim at reviving, repairing and redeveloping all those inaccessible or damaged but historically as well as culturally important literature across subjects so that the future generations may have an opportunity to study and learn from past works to embark upon a journey of creating a better future.

This book is a result of an effort made by Lector House towards making a contribution to the preservation and repair of original ancient works which might hold historical significance to the approach of continuous learning across subjects.

HAPPY READING & LEARNING!

LECTOR HOUSE LLP
E-MAIL: lectorpublishing@gmail.com